# **Contents**

# Discovering Iran

Iran, properly named The Islamic Republic of Iran, is about seven times the size of the UK and is located in the Middle East. It is a mountainous country known for its rich history and its strong economy, but also for its disagreements with other world powers, and some of its people complain of lack of freedom.

## The heart of the Middle East

Iran forms a gateway from neighbouring Iraq, Turkey and the Arab states to Central Asia in the east; and it has mountains and desert plains, and northern and southern coastlines. It has one of the strongest economies in the region, and its people are mostly educated and healthy. Many Iranians today live in cities, and the capital, Tehran, is flourishing.

## A long and stormy history

Iran is famous for its rich history and culture. Western people called the area Persia, after an empire that existed on and around the Iranian plateau, until around 330 BCE. In 1935, the government of Iran said that the name Iran should be used, as it was more popular with the local people.

This map shows Iran's major cities, its bordering countries and its coastlines.

**DID YOU KNOW?**
Iran's flag has the words 'Allah Akbar' ('God is Great') written in red in the centre, and these words are repeated 22 times in total along the top and bottom edges.

4

In 1979 the Islamic Revolution took place, and since then the country has been a theocratic republic, with a government run by religious leaders. These include a Supreme Leader and a President. The country has developed fast in the last 30 years, but relations with the rest of the world are often tense. In recent years Iran has frequently clashed with Western countries, especially the USA. Iran's development of uranium, for nuclear technology, has been the source of much tension, and other world powers have placed sanctions (or rules) on Iran.

## Election protests

During the 2009 presidential election it was announced that Mahmoud Ahmadinejad, who had been President since 2005, had won the majority of the vote. Many people believed that the election had not been carried out fairly. This led to the 2009-2010 Iranian election protests both within Iran and in major cities outside the country. The protests led to thousands of arrests and some deaths. The events have been nicknamed the 'Twitter Revolution' because many of the protesters used online social-networking sites to communicate with each other. In 2013, Hassan Rouhani was elected as President of Iran. His electoral victory has improved Iran's relations with other countries.

**Iran statistics**

**Area:** 1,648,195 sq km (636,372 sq miles)

**Capital city:** Tehran

**Government type:** Theocratic republic

**Bordering countries:** Afghanistan, Armenia, Azerbaijan-proper, Azerbaijan Naxcivan, Iraq, Pakistan, Turkey, Turkmenistan

**Currency:** Iranian rials (IRR)

**Language:** Persian and Persian dialects 58%, Turkic and Turkic dialects 26%, Kurdish 9%, Luri 2%, Balochi 1%, Arabic 1%, Turkish 1%, other 2%

▼ Many of Iran's bustling cities are situated below mountain ranges, as they depend on underground water channelled from deep inside the mountains.

# Landscape and climate

Iran mainly consists of a high desert plateau, surrounded by mountains, and bordered by Eastern Europe to the west, the Arabian Peninsula to the south-west, and Asia to the east. The Caspian Sea and the Persian Gulf (sea) border the north and south, and Iran also controls several islands in the Persian Gulf.

## A changeable climate

Weather varies throughout Iran. In the capital, Tehran, it is mainly mild and very similar to the UK in all four seasons. The surrounding north and west regions have clear seasons with extreme hot and cold temperatures, and snow on the mountains. The central desert region and the south are mainly mild in winter but hot and humid in summer, with high temperatures of 45 degrees Celsius in the southern city of Abadan.

**DID YOU KNOW?**
The highest mountain in Iran, Mount Damavand, standing at 5,671 m (18,606 feet), is also a volcano. It is said in one story to be the final resting place of Noah's Ark.

▼ The Elburz mountain range sits along the north of the Iranian plateau, and is made up of many, mostly inactive, volcanic peaks.

## High lands

Iran's high plateau of salt deserts and marshes is around 1,500 m (5,000 feet) above sea level. Two mountain ranges run along the north and south of Iran. Mount Taftan, in the southern Zagros mountains, still emits gas and mud from its volcanic cone. Iran also experiences dangerous earthquakes. In 2003 the city of Bam in the east was struck by a relatively mild earthquake, which still resulted in more than 25,000 deaths.

## Water sources

One-third of Iran's boundary is sea coast, but there is little surface water inland. There are some fertile valleys in Iran, but much of the land is dry wasteland, where irrigation from underground water is essential for farming. There is little rainfall, but snowfalls in mountainous areas feed the rivers every spring. The main rivers, including the longest river, the Safid, run from the two main mountain ranges to the seas. Lake Urmia, the largest lake, covers 5,180 sq km (2,000 sq miles).

▶ There are many small, seasonal streams in Iran, and villagers also use underground water from springs and wells.

### Facts at a glance

**Land area:** 1,531,595 sq km (591,352 sq miles)

**Water area:** 116,600 sq km (45,020 sq miles)

**Longest river:** Safid River 1,000 km (600 miles)

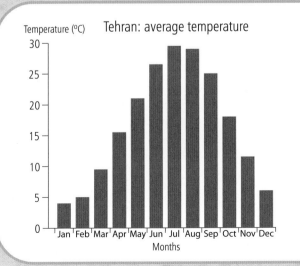

Temperature (°C)    Tehran: average temperature

Rainfall (mm)    Tehran: average rainfall

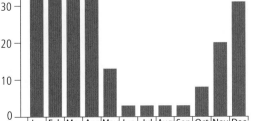

In 2009 Iran had a population of around 74 million, which was more than triple what it was 50 years ago. Iran's population is growing more slowly now, but still increasing by nearly a million every year.

## A mixed country

Different groups of people have been arriving and settling in the country since ancient times. Although the main ethnic group is mostly thought of as 'the Persian people', Persian speakers actually include other groups, such as Turkic, Arab and Kurd, and smaller minorities such as Armenians and Jews.

## Changing population

In the last 30 years, refugees and asylum seekers have arrived in Iran from war-torn countries nearby, including Afghanistan and Iraq. There are now nearly 1 million Afghan refugees in Iran. The government recently tightened its controls on incoming refugees, and there have been reports of people being deported, forced to relocate or held in camps, sometimes against international laws.

### Facts at a glance

**Total population:** 74.2 million

**Life expectancy at birth:** 71 years

**Children dying before the age of five:** 0.32%

**Ethnic composition:** Persian 51%, Azeri 24%, Gilaki and Mazandarani 8%, Kurd 7%, Arab 3%, Lur 2%, Baloch 2%, Turkic 2%, other 1%

▼ This refugee camp near Khoy holds over 50,000 Kurdish refugees from Iraq. The camp has been here since the 1970s, as new Kurdish refugees continue to arrive in Iran.

**DID YOU KNOW?**
On average, women live four years longer than men in Iran. A girl born in 2010 is expected to live 73 years, and a boy only 69 years.

◀ People protest in Sweden about an Iranian government election in 2009 that was declared unfair by international monitors. Some people choose to leave Iran to live in places where they feel they have more freedom.

## Health and life expectancy

The main causes of death in Iran are diseases and accidents. Healthcare in Iran is good, and water quality is better than in the rest of the region. A child born in Iran in 2010 is expected to live to 71 years of age, eight years less than a child born in the UK, and five years more than in neighbouring Pakistan. The average age in the country is around 27. As good healthcare allows this population to grow old, there will be more elderly people overall.

## Coping with more people

By 2050 the population in Iran is expected to reach nearly 100 million. This will mean larger, more heavily populated cities, and more people needing education, healthcare and employment. However, Iran has already coped with a rapidly increasing population, after the Revolution in 1979.

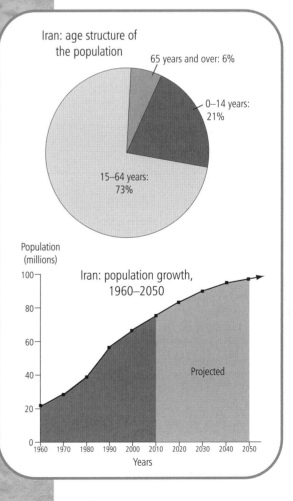

Iran: age structure of the population

65 years and over: 6%

0–14 years: 21%

15–64 years: 73%

Population (millions)

Iran: population growth, 1960–2050

Projected

Years

# Settlements and living

Iran is increasingly an urban country, and in 2009 more than 70 per cent of the population lived in cities. Most major cities are located in the low regions near the borders of Iran, where the climate and soil are better. It is usually only nomadic people who live in the harshest areas, moving around to find milder conditions.

## Cities

Around 7.9 million people live in Tehran, Iran's largest city and capital. Mashhad, the country's second-largest city, which is slightly larger than Birmingham, the UK's second city, is also a major urban centre. Cities in Iran are divided into different sections, and they have both modern skyscrapers and traditional central market areas, called bazaars, where people work and trade. Houses in urban areas often have a courtyard surrounded by a building, which stays cool on hot days. As the cities grew in the 1990s, housing for people on lower incomes was of a poorer quality. Since then, projects have been launched to improve the quality of houses for everyone in cities.

### Facts at a glance

**Urban population:** 70% (52 million)

**Rural population:** 30% (22.1 million)

**Population of largest city:** 7.9 million (Tehran)

▼ Urban life in Iran is very similar to that in other parts of the world. People enjoy going to coffee- and tea-shops, shopping and using mobile phones and MP3 players.

## Traditional housing

Many people in Iran still live in rural areas. The mosque often marks the centre of a village, and people go there to study as well as to worship. A typical village on the plains forms a rectangular pattern, with the mosque in the middle. In contrast, nomadic peoples such as the Turkmen and Baloch have more temporary housing, such as yurts (a kind of tent) or huts. In the mountains, mud-brick dwellings protect against the weather, whereas nearer the milder and more fertile Caspian Sea, two-storey houses are common, built with wood from the forest areas nearby.

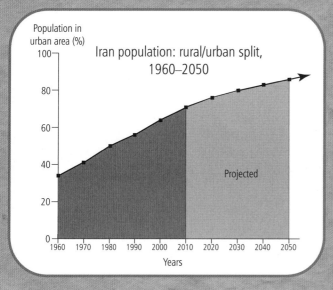

Population in urban area (%)

Iran population: rural/urban split, 1960–2050

Projected

Years

◐ Village houses are built using both traditional and modern techniques and materials, depending on the materials available and the local environment.

**DID YOU KNOW?**

Iran's cities are growing at a rate of nearly 3,000 people every day. By 2050, 86 per cent of Iranians will live in a city.

# Family life

The traditional family is still at the centre of life in Iran, but this is now beginning to change. Although the government prefers families to be headed by a man, often with several wives and children, young men and women in Iran today are campaigning for a more modern lifestyle.

## The role of the family

The Ayatollah Khomeini, who led the Islamic Revolution in 1979, encouraged people to plan smaller families, after a population surge caused problems with housing and healthcare in the 1980s. Now, the average number of children per family is 1.7 (instead of 6 or 7, as it was 30 years ago).

## Facts at a glance

**Average children per childbearing woman:**
1.7 children

**Average household size:**
4.1 people

▼ Many Iranian weddings follow the tradition shown here of a meal eaten outdoors.

▲ Families in Iran have been encouraged to leave time in between each child being born, and to have a maximum of three children, to help control the population.

## Children's lives

Most children in Iran go to school, but they also help with cooking, cleaning and other household chores. Rural children may help with farming work before and after school, or they might not attend school at all, especially in their teens. Some children also earn money in the cities, by shining shoes, cleaning windscreens or selling snacks.

## Women in Iran

The Iranian government controls news in Iran, so it is sometimes difficult to find out about life there, but both positive and negative stories emerge about Iranian women's lives. Unlike in most other countries, it is against the law for a woman to have a relationship with a man unless she is married to him. Some women have been lashed, and sentenced to death by stoning, for having a relationship with a man, especially if they are already married to someone else. Women are legally obliged to cover their hair and dress modestly, and can also be punished for disobeying this law.

**DID YOU KNOW?** Most Iranian girls used to get married at about 14. Since 1980, the average age has risen to around 21, but more and more women are choosing not to marry at all.

# Religion and beliefs

Religion is central to everyday life in Iran. A total of 89 per cent of Iranians are Shia Muslims, but globally the Shia branch is a minority in Islam. Shia and Sunni Muslims separated in the seventh and eighth centuries because of many disagreements about who should become caliph or religious leader, after the death of the Prophet Muhammad in 632 CE.

## Theocratic republic

Iran was declared an Islamic Republic during the Revolution in 1979, and immediately strict laws were passed, banning alcohol and Western music and controlling women's dress and behaviour.

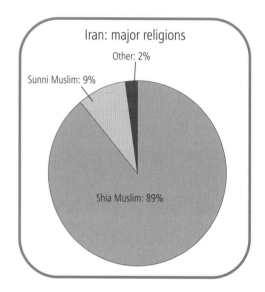

Iran: major religions

Other: 2%
Sunni Muslim: 9%
Shia Muslim: 89%

▼ Male and female followers of Islam worship separately, in different areas of mosques.

The Islamic Republic of Iran is still governed by a (male) Supreme Leader and a group of clerics or scholars, who have studied Shi'ism. A man can be given the title of scholar or cleric if the rest of the clergy believe he understands the religion well enough to lead. Iran is the only Islamic state in the world with this type of government. The ruling clerics in the Assembly of Experts in Iran decide laws, justice and the sentences for crimes, all based on traditional Sharia law, which is said to follow the will of Allah (God).

## Other beliefs in Iran

Although Islam is the main faith, there are also Christians, Jews and Zoroastrians living in Iran. Zoroastrianism is an Iranian religion from the time of the ancient Greeks, which combines belief in one God with magic and astrology. There are also followers of the Bahá'í faith, a religion that started in Iran in 1844. Bahá'ís believe in combining all world religions, and that every religious leader in the world has been God in human form. Three places in government, out of 290, are reserved for leaders of religious minorities.

These buildings in the ancient city of Yazd, with their domes, arches and towers, are beautiful examples of Islamic architecture.

**DID YOU KNOW?**
Karbala, a 680 CE battle in Iraq, in which Shias were killed in their fight to decide the caliph, is commemorated every year. Iranians show respect by fasting, and men beat themselves in the streets.

# Education and learning

Most children in Iran go to school, and boys and girls are taught separately. People in Iran are generally more educated than in the neighbouring countries of Pakistan and Afghanistan. Students complete their studies at universities and colleges, or they can study a vocational course such as business or agriculture. Learning about Islam is a large part of education.

## Mosque school

Children attend primary school, and over 30 per cent go to secondary school. At mosque schools, called madrassahs, children learn about the five pillars of Islam: to declare your belief, to pray, to fast during Ramadan, to pay a religious tax, and to complete a pilgrimage or hajj to Mecca during your lifetime.

## Learning in the army

All young males in Iran must do 18 months of military service from the age of 19, although boys can join some forces when they are only 15. Strict education continues for these soldiers. The military aims to make sure that Iran stays an Islamic Republic, and trains soldiers to help the Iranian people follow its laws.

⬤ This boy is completing his homework outside his father's shop in Esfahan. Children in Iran attend primary school, then middle school from 11 years old, and then secondary school, from 14 to 17 years of age.

### Facts at a glance

**Children in primary school:**
Male 91%, Female 100%
**Children in secondary school:**
Male 45%, Female 32%
**Literacy rate (over 15 years):**
77%

## Universities

After the revolution many university lecturers had to leave their jobs in Iran because they did not support the government. Because of this, there are not enough university teachers, and Iranians often go to university overseas.

Some Iranians choose to stay in countries with less strict laws. Educated people have had problems in Iran ever since the revolution, and earlier, because they have often wanted the country to modernise its laws and their views are against those of the government. University education in Iran is improving, and there are many courses available. Most graduates specialise in humanities and engineering.

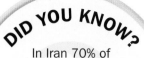

**DID YOU KNOW?**

In Iran 70% of women can read and write, compared to only 36% of women in Pakistan.

▼ In one project in Iran, according to UNICEF, some schools are running weekly after-school classes with the schoolgirls themselves supervising the activities.

# Employment and economy

Iran holds about 10 per cent of the world's oil reserves (oil lying underground), and in the last 30 years its economy has grown and shrunk alongside the global price of oil. The oil industry has brought wealth and jobs to Iran, but not everyone shares these benefits.

## Money and independence

When the revolutionary government came to power in 1979 it was unhappy with Iran's close links with the USA and it set about making Iran economically independent. This led to more employment opportunities and many people left rural farming areas to seek jobs in cities.

### Facts at a glance

**Contributions to GDP:**
  agriculture: 11%
  industry: 45%
  services: 44%
**Labour force:**
  agriculture: 25%
  industry: 31%
  services: 44%
**Female labour force:**
  30% of total
**Unemployment rate:** 12%

▼ Small-scale farmers sell their produce at a local market in southern Iran.

## Jobs and services

Today only a quarter of working Iranians farm (compared to about 40 per cent in 1979), and about a third do industrial work in factories, oil production or mining. The service sector provides the most jobs, including teachers', nurses' and shop assistants' posts. The government is a large employer, as it owns the banks, insurance companies, energy and water companies, as well as the telephone and television companies.

About a third of women (more than in many other Middle Eastern nations) are employed and this proportion is increasing. However, women still suffer many inequalities, including lower pay, fewer workers' rights, and some harassment.

## Unemployment

Iran's unemployment rate is 12 per cent, which is higher than in the USA, India and the UK. Some Iranians are very poorly paid and, between 1990 and 2005, 7 per cent of the population was living on less than US$2 (about £1.20) a day. The Ministry of Welfare is in charge of reducing poverty, and recent reforms are bringing in new cash payments for the poorer members of Iran's population, but some welfare experts in Iran say that the government should do more. Many educated Iranians leave Iran to work in other countries, in search of a better quality of life.

⚫ Women at work in the Iranian interior ministry in Tehran.

**DID YOU KNOW?**

Unlike banks in Western countries, banks in Iran are banned from charging fees on money borrowed from them, because it is against the religion of Islam.

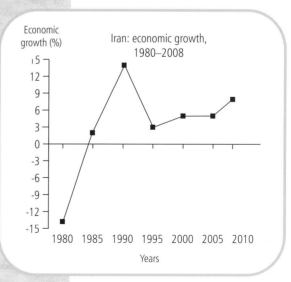

Iran: economic growth, 1980–2008

Economic growth (%)

Years

# Industry and trade

Iran has avoided trading with wealthy Western countries such as the USA since the Islamic Revolution. It only trades with certain countries nearby in the region, such as the United Arab Emirates (UAE), or other world powers that also stand independent of the USA.

## The energy industry

Iran is the world's second-largest producer of oil and natural gas. The country also produces more electricity than it needs. The government-controlled National Iranian Oil Company supervises most petroleum extraction and many oil refineries near major cities in Iran.

▼ An Iranian oil storage facility is overshadowed by vast mountains. Iran also stores its crude oil in a fleet of supertankers in the Persian Gulf.

▶ This woman is weaving a Persian carpet, which is an important Iranian export still popular throughout the world as a symbol of Persian history. There are an estimated 1.2 million carpet weavers in Iran.

## Local industry

Manufacturing in Iran has grown in the last 50 years, and it now produces a wide range of items, including cars, electrical appliances, phones, machinery, paper, rubber products, steel, food products, wood and leather goods, textiles and pharmaceuticals. Most of these goods are sold in the major cities.

## Trading

Iran has become more independent from Western countries in the last 30 years, but Iranians still need to import many items. These vary from food products to manufactured goods, although some cultural items, such as Western music and films, are banned. As well as Iran's main export, oil, it also exports fruit, nuts and crafts.

## International problems

There has been a major disagreement between the Iranian government and other nations about Iran's nuclear capability. The government of Iran says it is developing nuclear technology for use in generating energy for the Iranian people, but some countries, such as the USA and the UK, fear that Iran is developing nuclear weapons.

Iran has also been accused of supporting Hezbollah and the Taliban, two terrorist groups that have been responsible for the deaths of many civilians in countries across the world. This possible link with international terrorism has led Western nations to enforce more sanctions against Iran, making trade very difficult.

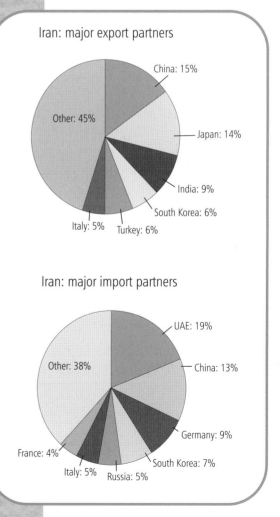

Iran: major export partners

China: 15%
Japan: 14%
India: 9%
South Korea: 6%
Turkey: 6%
Italy: 5%
Other: 45%

Iran: major import partners

UAE: 19%
China: 13%
Germany: 9%
South Korea: 7%
Russia: 5%
Italy: 5%
France: 4%
Other: 38%

# Farming and food

Farming in Iran now produces 11 per cent of the country's national income. Although far fewer people farm now than they did 30 years ago, Iran still relies on locally produced food, and some luxury crops are important national exports.

## Rural decline

Much of Iran's soil is poor, making large-scale farming difficult. In addition, farms are often small and family-run, and therefore not very profitable. These are some of the reasons why many people have left farms to find work in urban areas.

### Facts at a glance

**Farmland as % of total land area:** 30%

**Main agricultural exports:** pistachios, raisins, dates, wheat

**Main agricultural imports:** maize, soy bean oil, palm oil, rice, sugar

**Average daily calorie intake:** 3040

▼ Farm workers near Astara, on the coast of the Caspian Sea, harvest rice using traditional tools.

## Fishing

Fishing is popular on both coastlines, and in the Caspian Sea sturgeon are caught because their eggs (known as caviar) are a highly prized luxury food. The sturgeon are traditionally wild, although they are now sometimes farmed. Their eggs are extracted and the fish are often re-released afterwards, to produce more roe, or eggs. Caviar is a key export for Iran.

## Many crops

Most of the food produced in Iran is sold within the country. Very little food is exported, and only a small amount is imported. Main crops include cereals such as wheat, barley, rice and maize; fruits such as dates, figs, pomegranates, melons and grapes; and vegetables. Cotton is also grown, as well as sugar beets and sugar cane, nuts, olives, spices, tea, tobacco and medicinal herbs.

## Iranian food

Herding is also an important part of Iranian life and dairy products (mostly made from the milk of sheep and goats) are central to the Iranian diet. Food varies in the different regions, but rice and flatbreads are eaten everywhere. Meat, mostly lamb, is common, often eaten in a stew flavoured with herbs such as mint and spices such as saffron and turmeric. Alcohol is forbidden in Iran, but tea served black in glasses is popular, and seasonal fruit is often eaten.

Tea served in the traditional style in a glass (*ormud*), with a dish of pastries, presented on a small patterned cloth (*qalamkar*).

# Transport and communications

Transport and communications in Iran have been modernised in the last 20 years. As in other countries, people fly, and use mobile phones and social networking media, but these are all largely controlled by the Iranian government. Iranians therefore have limited freedom to communicate and travel.

## Communication and censorship

Mobile phone ownership in Iran has almost doubled in the last three years. There are also more Internet users now. These developments have eased the flow of information between Iran and the rest of the world. But the Iranian government believes that Western ideas are damaging to Iranians. It therefore censors Internet communication, and stops some mobile phone videos being sent.

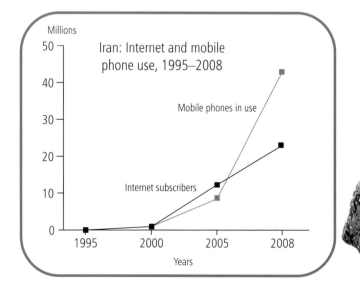

Iran: Internet and mobile phone use, 1995–2008

Millions

Mobile phones in use

Internet subscribers

Years

▶ More than one in four people now own a mobile phone in Iran.

This is quite easy for the government, as it owns or controls most newspapers, TV news channels and the national email service. Sometimes the Iranian government stops people such as journalists and human rights workers from travelling to, or within, Iran.

## Transport in Iran

Iran's mountainous and desert areas make travelling difficult. Buses and trucks carry people and cargo between the main cities, and boats are used on the large River Karun. Iran Air provides flights between cities, as well as to many international destinations. Railways also link the major cities and are used by some to travel through the country from Middle East states to Central Asia.

## Urban transport

The main cities have their own bus networks, and Tehran has a subway system with several lines. As the cities have grown, the number of cars has increased rapidly, as it has elsewhere in the world, causing traffic problems. In 2010 the Iranian government started trying to reduce the traffic and air pollution by giving people incentives to move to other cities.

▶ Traffic is becoming a problem in Tehran, shown here in the distance, but overall car ownership is still quite low in Iran, compared to the UK or China.

# Leisure and tourism

As Iranians in the cities become wealthier, they have more money to spend on leisure activities such as going to the cinema and playing sport. International tourists also come to Iran, and in 2008 over two million people visited Iran's tourist attractions.

## Persian history

Iran is famous for its Persian Empire, which ended when the Persians were conquered by Alexander the Great in the fourth century. There are now 12 World Heritage sites in Iran, including the two capitals of the former empire, Persepolis and Pasargadae. They contain ruins of grand buildings and homes from the sixth and seventh centuries BCE.

▼ Many tourists go to Iran each year to visit ruins from the Persian Empire, such as these columns in the ancient city of Persepolis.

Some sites are even older, dating back to the Mesopotamian Empire and the Kingdom of Elam (other ancient civilisations partly located in Iran). Tourists visit these historic sites but also enjoy Iran's beaches, ski resorts and beautiful mosques.

## Celebration

Iran's main day of celebration is Nowruz, the New Year holiday, and the birthday of the twelfth Imam. Nowruz is celebrated with a week's holiday, ending with a picnic. On the night before the last Wednesday of the old year, called Red Wednesday, people leap over bonfires to cast out the ill omens of the old year.

▼ People enjoy boating on the Zayandeh River in Esfahan during the national holiday of Nowruz.

## Culture

Iranian-made films have been praised by critics around the world. The government has not been able to control the film industry, but it does try to limit the films that are produced. The government is in favour of films that celebrate Iranian life. Films that seem too close to Western life or too critical of Iranian life are not officially screened in the country.

Sport, both traditional and modern, is also popular with Iranians. Many cheered on the Iranian football team in the 2010 World Cup, and football is widely played and watched. Traditional sports include wrestling and horse racing.

**DID YOU KNOW?**
TV in Iran is popular, but watching non-government TV is difficult, as international channels like BBC Persia are often jammed or blocked to stop Iranians watching them.

# Environment and wildlife

As Iran has developed, people's behaviour has begun to have more impact on wildlife and the environment. The government is taking some steps to prevent this, but international experts advise countries like Iran, with developing economies, to invest in more renewable energy to avoid contributing to global $CO_2$ emissions.

## Environmental damage

Air pollution affects Iran's cities, and as fuel is so easy for the country to access, the people of Iran have less motivation to reduce their car usage. Electricity use has more than doubled in the last 15 years, and most of this comes from oil-burning power stations, releasing more $CO_2$ and pollution into the atmosphere.

Air pollution in Tehran sometimes rises to dangerous levels, causing offices and schools to close.

## Wildlife

A huge variety of plants and animals exist in Iran, and different species live in each region. In desert areas there are shrubs and bushes, and oases where date palms and acacia trees grow. Desert animals include rabbits, deer, onagers (a kind of desert horse) and rodents, as well as birds of prey such as buzzards. In the mountains and forests there are leopards, hyenas, bears, wild boars and gazelles. Sea birds live along the coastal areas and over 200 varieties of fish and some shellfish live in the Persian Gulf.

## Protection

There were once tigers in Iran, but they are now thought to be extinct. The government has established National Parks and Protected Areas to protect the wildlife of Iran. Endangered species include the salamander and, in the Caspian region, the rare Asian cheetah. The government has also banned the hunting of some species such as swans, deer and pheasants.

The onager is still found in Iran's deserts but it is now critically endangered.

**DID YOU KNOW?**
It is thought that there are only 100 Asian cheetahs left in the wild in Iran. In ancient times cheetahs were trained by kings to hunt gazelles.

# Glossary

**ayatollah** important religious leader for Shia Muslims

**campaigning** working towards achieving a goal, especially a change in something

**censor** examine books, films, TV and newspapers and cut out parts that have ideas, beliefs or messages that are believed to be unacceptable

**censorship** the process of censoring books, films, TV and newspapers and other media, usually carried out by officials

**cleric** a religious leader who has studied religion closely, and who people believe is educated and wise

**commemorate** honour a memory by holding a ceremony or event

**deport** force somebody to leave a country, especially if they are a foreigner

**emit** produce or let out a gas or other substance

**herding** keeping and looking after livestock, such as sheep and goats

**incentive** a reason, or reward, for doing something

**manufacturing** making something or many things, using machinery

**military** the armed forces in a country

**minorities** small groups of people within a country, who are different in some way from the main population of the country

**nomadic** moving around throughout the year, rather than living in one place permanently, often to farm animals in the best climate and condition by moving them from place to place

**nuclear technology** the science and materials needed to develop nuclear energy or nuclear weapons

**peninsula** a piece of land projecting out into the sea

**petroleum extraction** process of removing petroleum or oil from rock beds under the ground or sea

**pilgrimage** a journey to a place that is important in a person's religion

**plateau** an area of fairly flat high ground

**procession** many people or vehicles moving together on a route as part of a ceremony

**Ramadan** the ninth and holiest month of the Islamic calendar, during which people fast and pray

**revolution** the overthrow of a government to make way for a new system or ruler

**sanction** measure taken by one country to try and make another country comply with international agreements and laws

# Topic web

Use this topic web to explore Iranian themes
in different areas of your curriculum.

**Citizenship**

Do you think that people in Iran have the same rights as people in the UK? What are the main differences? Can you think of anything that people in Iran are not allowed to do, that people in the UK are free to do?

**ICT**

Imagine that you want to visit Iran on a tourist trip. Use the Internet to find out which attractions you should visit, and when you should go.

**History**

Find out about how people lived in one of the ancient empires that Iran is famous for. You could choose Persia, Mesopotamia or the Kingdom of Elam.

**Design and Technology**

Use the information on housing in villages in Iran to make some models of the different types of village house.

**Iran**

**Maths**

Iran's currency is the rial. Find out how many rials there are in £1, £5 and £10.

**Science**

Extracting and refining oil or petroleum is Iran's main industry. Find out what solids, liquids and gases are involved in the oil extraction and refining processes.

**English**

Using pages 28–9 on 'Environment and wildlife', design and write an information factsheet describing the main animals and birds in Iran, and use the Internet to find out more facts to include.

**Geography**

Iran is a country in the heart of the Middle East, with many different border countries. Use a map to work out which parts of Iran are close to Europe, and which to the Middle East and Asia.

# Further information and index

## Further reading

*Iran and the West* (Our World Divided), Philip Steele (Wayland 2011)
*Iran* (Changing World), Richard Dargle (Watts 2008)
*Iran* (Looking at Countries), Kathleen Pohl (Watts 2008)
*Iran* (Welcome to my Country), D Yip, M O'Shea (Watts 2005)

## Web

*https://www.cia.gov/library/publications/the-world-factbook/geos/ir.html*
Key statistics about Iran's landscape, population, economy, government and more.
*http://news.bbc.co.uk/1/hi/790877.stm*
Country profile on Iran, with key facts and links to other Iran websites.
*http://www.guardian.co.uk/world/iran*
Country profile, plus all the latest news on Iran.

## Index